Praise for Jason Ryberg

"Jason Ryberg's poems ought to be tackled in front of a plate of runny eggs and hashbrowns, late night in some greasy spoon diner where you can still smoke cigarettes, where truck drivers and salesmen with briefcases full of drugs and lewd secrets and the murderers from Capote's *In Cold Blood* all might stop to eat on the same night, under a moon *like the atomically radiant skull / of a bald and diabolical clown*. His books should come pre-worn, covers already tattered and stained with unidentified life fluids, favorite pages scribbled on and half-loosed from the binding. Each of Ryberg's lines should be read in a gargle-y, Tom Waitsian rumble that embodies the boogey-men that hide inside his images. Folks, this stuff is weird, wild. And even better, this stuff is good."

-Justin Hamm, *The Inheritance: Poems and Photographs*

"With *Standing at the Intersection of Critical Mass and Event Horizon* Jason Ryberg returns with another satisfying collection of sturdy and unpretentious poems. Rooted in the earth of the Midwest, these eloquent, plain-spoken considerations of everyday life are like sitting with a friend over coffee in a diner as he explains about the darkness lurking beneath the light and the profound light hidden within our darkness."

-Michael J. Arcangelini, *What the Night Keeps*
(Stubborn Mule Press)

"How does an everyday person, an EveryOne, deal with it all and still maintain a sense of self (and of normalcy), despite the omnipresence of divisive news? An EveryOne cannot freeze with outrage and bewilderment every time the internet or the news updates and intrudes. An EveryOne must work, eat, breathe, and find a way to keep the neighborhood peace and make sense of it all. In keeping with this, in his new collection of poems *Standing At the Intersection of Critical Mass and Event Horizon,* Kansas poet Jason Ryberg gives voice to this contemporary EveryOne. Written in a direct imagistic style which is both philosophical and funny, Ryberg's poems lay out the poet's own struggle between self and society. In doing so, he lends the reader a sense of peace as he has found it.."

  -Michael Hathaway, publisher, *Chiron Review*

"*Standing at the Intersection of Critical Mass and Event Horizon* is an extraordinary journey through the mindset and cosmic experience of today's independent American citizen, lost in a corrupt and leaderless society yet in love with the beauty of the universe—and connected to all corners and corridors of history and space and time through a hyperlinked anxiety. This is a rich tapestry of complex shapes and shades, which only a poet of Jason Ryberg's insight and experience could lead us through."

  -Jared Smith, *That's How It Is* (Stubborn Mule Press)

"Although his life and work is deeply rooted in the get-by-as-best-you-can blue collar world of the American Midwest, Jason Ryberg reminds of the ancient Chinese poets through his impossibly long titles and through his playful focus on friendship and place. His poetry combines the odd and the everyday, the outsider and the neighbor. He commiserates with, *hobo clowns/who dreamed, foolishly, of being poets /of all things.* At the same time he can step away and pass the, *that high-test grade of silence.*"

  -Mike James, author of *Jumping Drawbridges in Technicolor and Parades*

STANDING AT THE INTERSECTION OF CRITICAL MASS AND EVENT HORIZON

POEMS (OLD AND NEW) BY
JASON RYBERG

Luchador Press
Big Tuna, TX

Copyright © Jason Ryberg, 2019
First Edition1 3 5 7 9 10 8 6 4 2
ISBN: 978-1-950380-16-9
LCCN: 2019903144

Cover image: Jon Lee Grafton
Title page image: Will Leathem
Author photo:: Jeanette Powers
All rights reserved. No part of this publication may be reproduced or transmitted in any form or by any means, electronic or mechanical, including photocopying, recording or by info retrieval system, without prior written permission from the author.

The author would like to thank the editors of these publications where some of the poems in this collection first appeared (in some form or another):

Hobo Camp Review, Up The Staircase Quarterly, Blue Island Review, Clockwise Cat, Debris Magazine, The Poetry Warrior, Carcinogenic Poetry, Main Street Rag, Underground Voices, Primal Urge, Eviscerator Heaven, Inclement, Anger Management, Dark Lady Poetry, b.ak.tun magazine, Unquiet Desperation, Downgo Sun Magazine, Off Beat Pulp, The Toronto Quarterly, Gutter Elequence, The Meth Lab, Ann Arbor Review, Red Fez, The Screech Owl, pornSad, Bluest Aye, Words Dance , Message In A Bottle, Poetry Bay, Handful of Dust, Lucid Moon, Lung, As Well As Magazine, Mid-Western Gothic, Horror, Sleaze, Trash, Thunder Sandwich, The Greensilk Journal, Common Line Project, Crack the Spine, Kleft Jaw, South Broadway Ghost Society

Special thanks to El Dopa, Namoi Shupp-Pavey, the Osage Arts Community and the Aaron Morrison Home for Wayward Middle-Aged Men.

This book is dedicated to John and Melinda Ryberg.

TABLE OF CONTENTS

Scenes From 39th St., Pt. 1 / 1
A Tiny Drop of Truth / 3
The Universe Does Provide / 5
Bigger Than Life / 7
Consulting the Stars With Mark Hennessy / 10
Catching a Whiff / 12
This Poem is Mocking You / 14
Chet Baker Begins to Bleed / 18
Centering Your Chakra / 21
Drunk Directing Traffic at the Intersection
   of Time and Space / 24
The Night Before Payday (and Exactly
   Five Dollars in Quarters to Your Name) / 26
Standing at the Intersection of
   Critical Mass and Event Horizon
   with Tom Wayne and John Deuser,
   5:47am (or, Hey Man, is That an
   Accordian I'm Hearing?) / 27
Snowflakes / 29
Sleep During Thunderstorms / 33
The Great Who Knows / 34
Goat Piss Into Gasoline (or, the Poet
   Tries a Tiny Dab of Ms. Walsh's Bold
   and Spicy Sauce) / 35
Still-Life With Dragonfly Perched on Beer Bottle / 37
I Can Never Remember Exactly / 39

Charles Simic Sitting in the Cheap Seats
   of My Dreams / 41
Tomatoes / 43
Mean Boy Looking for His Gun
  (or, Portrait of the Word as
  Muse, Master and Estranged,
  Non-Gender-Specific Lover) / 46
Chance Meeting, 3am / 49
Madame Laveau, Fortune Teller and
  Police Psychic, Begins to See the Light / 50
Scenes From 39th St. Part 2 / 52
It / 56
In Which Monkey-Boy Attempts
  to Go Toe-to-Toe With the Master
  (Round 1) / 60
A Day on the Farm, Pt. 1 / 63
Every Other Thing / 64
The Story, So Far / 66
Whatever It Is / 68
My Generalized Other / 71
Madame Laveau, Fortune Teller
  and Police Psychic, Hands Out
  a Little Free Advice / 73
Pissing off the Back Porch (or,
  Golden Light in the Shadow
  of the Coming Darkness) / 75

Kansas Clouds / 79
Big Shots, Bagmen and Nobodies
   (or, the Day Dickey Grabbed
   the Red Phone) / 80
Son of It / 84
I Swear to God / 86
Burlap, Buffalo Skull and Burial Suit / 87
A Laughing Matter / 88
And Still the Moon / 92
Wherever They Stopped / 94
Mr. Heartlander, U.S.A. / 96
Fine Day in America, Sir / 97
A Day on the Farm, Pt. 2, / 99
In Which Monkey-Boy Attempts
   to Go Toe-to-Toe With the Master
   (Round 2) / 100
Return of It / 103
Open Letter to Lucas Jackson / 106
Wherein *It* Conquers the World / 107
Whatever *It* Was / 109
Consolation Prize / 110
Portrait of Old Man Smoking Cigarettes
   and Drinking Beer While Listening to the
   Cardinals / Royals Game on the Radio / 111
Grandeur / 112
Just Like That / 113
My Shoes, My Belt or My Haircut
   Never Got Me Laid / 115

LA-Z-BOY on the Front Porch / 117

Death Motif / 118

Your Sacrifices Are Greatly Appreciated / 120

Still-Life of Pocket Knife, Carpenter's Pencil
   and Black Velvet Elvis / 121

The Kind of Weed / 122

Preoccupied / 123

Gas Station Famous / 124

*History is a cookbook. The tyrants are chefs.
The philosophers write menus. The priests are waiters.
The military men are bouncers. The singing you hear
is the poets washing dishes in the kitchen.*

—Charles Simic, *The Monster Loves His Labyrinth*

Scenes From 39th St., Pt. 1

The Poet With the Hole in His Throat
was busy soaking copies of *Black Like Me*
in gasoline, shouting *I told you crackers*
what I'd do the next time I saw one of these things!
And the **Eastern Academic Elitist Poet**
(from (eastern-most) Hoboken) was
attempting to set Tennyson's *Charge Of*
the Light Brigade to jew's harp, tone box and oboe.
And the ferocious **Celtic / Valkyrie Poet**
was feasting on the still-beating hearts
of all the fallen poets foolish enough
to have fallen for her Celtic siren song.
And **God's Angry Poet** was casting out
the under-cover **Homeland Security Man**
with Lillies of the Field and various
lyrical incantations and the street preachers
were ladeling snake oil from a fifty-gallon drum
while some faintly unwholesome character
claiming to be the latest incarnation of the Bodhisattva
was saying to everyone and anyone on the street
HEY, PULL MY FINGER! PULL MY FINGER!
And then the ten-thousand myriad archetypes
became strangely quiet and still, the stars all stopped,
momentarily, in their places and the angels
and demons ceased their square-dancing on the heads
of pins and ten penny nails, everywhere.

And still the Lonely Backwoods Bukowski-
Wanna-Be Poet sat there in a dank sub-basement
corner of his imagination, mindlessly ringing
wind chimes made from throwing stars, winding
and re-winding the ancient mechanical cricket of his art.

A Tiny Drop of Truth

Sometimes the summer night's hot whisper
is nothing more than a black snake's hiss of a word
we cannot always quite discern-

a momentary corridor
of connectivity between us
and the outer darkness
between the stars-

a smooth shiny pebble of a word
barely graspable in its hard
slippery-slopish-ness,

nearly as ethereal on its surface
as the thought
at its dark heart,

a thought with a tiny drop of truth
in its blood, like a poison,
secretly insinuated into
the winding stream of things
in an attempt to stimulate some sort of healing
of the tear between the way things appear to be
and the way things really are,

a truth that by fevering up the blood a bit
and disquieting deep dreams
and maybe thereby prying open the inner onion-eye
that sleeps, deeply, at the center of the mind
forces itself

to at least be disbelieved.

The Universe Does Provide

for Steve Bridgens

Even after the sun
has long since gone down,
the brutal, kiln-like intensity
of a day like today
(here, in this overgrown cow town
in late July) can still be felt
well into the night.

The sidewalks and driveways
and newly resurfaced streets
continue to throw off enough heat,
all our overgrown yards enough jungle steam
(due to a brief, but mean, little thunderstorm
this morning that not even
the weatherman had foreseen)
that our clankity old window-unit
is forced to shift down a few degrees
into a lower, more determined gear.

Still, something has called us all out here
to the front porch, tonight:

Maybe those recent reports of lightning on the horizon?
Constellations of fireflies churning before our eyes?

The tidal pull of a fat, blood orange of a moon?
Or, just the inevitable madness of tiny rooms?

All we really need to know
(here on this not-so-disagreeable night
in Kansas City, KS in late July)
is there's an hour of Mingus
coming up on the community radio,
a fridge full of beer getting colder and colder
and a one-hitter already loaded up for you
and ready to go.

So, even though we all got jobs
that come calling way too early in the morning
and bills and debts that, over time, seem to have become
highly resistant to our attempts at neutralizing them
and despite all the headlines and sound bites
(detailing the latest home-grown inanity
or gruesome instance of international mayhem)
that appear to be conspiring to reinforce
the near-blasphemous notion that can
so easily lead one to believe otherwise,

from time to time

the universe does provide.

Bigger Than Life
for Will Leathem

Here we are, brothers and sisters,

little lost lambs at play in elysian fields of corn
(slated to be transformed
into a tarmacked parking lot
and uber-mega-mall for the Lord).

Yes, here we are
beneath a vast, expansive canopy
of Big American Sky,

beneath criss-crossing contrails and cop-copters
and ever-multiplying spy satellites.

And here, at the clogged and burning heart
of doubled-up clusters of knotted six-lane highway
that twist and trail and snake away
off into meaningless meandering sentences
scrawled into a faceless landscape,

a bounty of boundless suburban sprawl
where, these days, it's all strip-malls,
corporate franchises and blackly bubblin' asphalt,
strip-searched and mined of every grain,
tid-bit and least divisible unit of soul,

where now, with frenzied, slicing, intercising
intersections, terraces, courts, cul-de-sacs
and roundabouts and all,
we are suddenly hobbled to a crawl
on our (less and less than merry) way
to yet another sub-suburban
subdivision of Nowheresville, USA.

But then, suddenly,
out of this strangely beautiful non-place
none of us could have ever expected
(that some higher power surely must have contracted,
specifically, for our limitless enjoyment and use),
somewhere along good ol' US 82,

a solitary hawk
perched on a buckshot-riddled
speed limit sign,

a cross made of flowers and ribbons
by the side of the road
(R.I.P Betty Mae Stokes,
You Will Be Missed And Loved, Always),

and there, quickly approaching on our right,
just this side of the last place of rest for the rest of our lives,
the pouty, petulant lips of a trailer-park princess
gone porn star queen,

beaming down, almost beatifically,
from a roadside billboard,

bigger than life,

promising us (for the right price, anyway)
the heart and soul
and credit card number
of America.

Consulting the Stars
with Mark Hennessy

And then there are those
wide-open October nights
out there on the high seas
of the lower Midwest,

and nothing but stars   stars   stars.

And maybe you've wandered
away from the fire with a friend or two
and a bottle of some not dissimilar
distillation of heat and radiance (to keep
the Universal Engine turning over, of course),

and Time, that supremely indifferent
retriever and reducer of all things
to their least divisible units
seems to have momentarily halted
in the tracks of its ceaseless stalking
of what we so self-centrically
imagine to be its sweetest, juiciest prey.

And a Greek chorus of coyotes
is commenting on the day's events
all the way from the next county over.

And a truck out beyond
the horizon's line of
ever-diminishing returns
blows a long, sorrowful solo
just for us (or anybody else
who may be listening).

And our phones and clocks
(those little sycophantic servants,
advisers and grand co-conspirators,
as well, no doubt) have been given
their first night off
in who knows how long.

So, if you want to speak to someone,
present company should more than do.

And if, for some reason,
you find you need to know
the Time's current whereabouts...

well, you'll have to consult the stars.

Catching a Whiff

This old
black dog

on this cold
black night,

ears that
sometimes hear

and only one
good eye

but, a stout
snout that still
sniffs, deeply, the truth
from many things

and with which
he now attempts
to catch the tail
of a whiff

of some
fleeting something

wafting along
on the cold
black wind

on this cold
black
night.

This Poem is Mocking You
for Bob Savino

This poem
starts from a postcard
from a place that no longer exists
(found in a book, never finished):
the book: Boccaccio's *Decameron*,
the postcard: *A View of Mainstreet, Studley, KS*,
Boccaccio: whereabouts unknown,
Studley, KS: a hundred years beneath a lake.

This poem
will have cold pizza
and orange juice for breakfast,
followed by three steep cups
of gritty, black atomic mud
while sifting through
John Lee Hooker's blues,
the 1952 *Farmer's Almanac*,
Lowrider Magazine
and the local classifieds

for something new to chew on,
something to stoke the Languishing Ember of Hope,
something to clip out and keep
in its musty scrapbook of a brain,
something to fly on the end of a string
in the middle of a wicked summer thunderstorm.

This poem will slowly begin
to accumulate strange names
and phone numbers in its pockets,
coffee stains in its margins,
wrinkles in its face and
stress fractures in its logic.

This poem will be wadded up
and banished from the court,
mauled by a one-eyed, three-legged tomcat
named Lucky Ned,
rescued, reconstructed and rehabilitated,
then put back in the running
with a new lease on life.

Later, upon closer examination,
It will be discovered
to have developed night vision
and a website with no domain.

This poem
will break its chain
and jump the fence
to wander and snuffle freely
through the dark, haunted forests
of young girls' dreams.

This poem
will pay fines for pissing
on The Washington Monument,

Grant's Tomb, The Alamo,
The George Brett Super Highway
and The Ronald Reagan Memorial something-or-other.

This poem
will do time for attempting to bribe public officials,
release itself on its own recognizance
and go joyriding in a '62 purple Impala,
(returning it unharmed at dawn).

This poem
will have itself forwarded
to the Great Unknown,
be found in a bottle
on the shore of Galapagos
and leave a near-identical copy of itself
to ride out the rest of the 21st century
folded up in the inside left breast pocket
of Joe Bannano's overcoat.

This poem will saturate the matrix
and circle the globe,
seemingly unnoticed.

Then, finally, when it's used up
all its privileges and favors,
made too many of the wrong enemies,
burned too many bridges
and racked up way too much debt,

It will unexpectedly erupt
into an unfathomable mushroom cloud
of chain letters, computer viruses
and nagging late-night suspicions,

leaving the world
radically altered,
forever.

More or less.

Chet Baker Begins to Bleed

There's grinning ghost-poets
riding fancy saddles
down abandoned hotel hallways,

a red rooster
wrestling a baby kingsnake,

a cat caught in the hen house
and a shiftless, no-good drifter
cooling in the jailhouse.

There's a broken-down truck
afloat on an ocean of golden wheat
beneath a swirling coal-black sky.

There's a foolish old rowboat
sulking in the bed of a creek
that's long since run dry
(still waiting after all these years
for the creek to reappear).

And here's the part
where one of our own dearly departed
is carried down an inner-city street
on a swollen river of laughter and tears,
trumpets, tambourines and slide trombones,
farther and farther out, towards some still (as yet)
greater unknown.

And what about that mad Rasputin of a character
down in his subterranean lair,
sculpting zodiac animals from spirits
of fire and air?

And way up there, just above the city skyline,
goes the Man With All The Answers,
wafting away to some faraway land, most likely,
on a *deus ex machina* made of wanderlust,
bailing wire and gull's wings,

leaving us a world of mysteries
that may very well remain unanswered
forever more (*forever more... forever more...*   )

But then, before anyone can catch their breath, even,
comes the big budget, *WHAMMO!,* climactic scene
where the stadium floor of the world's latest
collective dream (of whatever's passing, these days,
for peace, love and understanding) suddenly blows
and drops out from beneath it all

and we tumble and fall,
tumble and fall,
tumble and fall,

like starfish,
like rag dolls,
like satellites spiraling, drunkenly,
out of their orbits,

off into the sleepy, wakening yawn
of a shimmering nebula, the stellar semblance
of a giant rose a million years wide
and the color of peach ice cream.

Somewhere, a pay phone
by the side of a desert highway
begins to ring.

Somewhere, a tattoo of Chet Baker
begins to bleed.

Centering Your Chakra

Nothing especially tragi-glamorous
or hardcore / blue collar / neo-beat
about cracking an egg into a beer
at 10:30 on a Tuesday morning while
watching the *700 Club*.

Nothing world-wearily decadent
or anti-romantically *nu-kowskian*
about not having filed a tax return
for who knows how many years, now.

Nothing in there that's gonna net you
an honorable mention (or even
a minor addendum) in anybody's rolls,
records or register of highly conspicuous
anti-social types (except maybe your own
(elaborately constructed), of course).

And it looks like it's a Schlitz Malt Liquor
Tall-Bull, this time, and maybe a pull off
the Old Overholt Rye (what some of us around
these parts like to call *Old Reach-Around*),
and all before I've even had my coffee
and / or some semblance of breakfast
(really, Mr. Ryberg, what can you be thinking?).

And, whereas I can fully understand
how and why my mother might not quite be able
to wrap her brain around this (only occasional and,
I suspect, primarily male) ritual and might even
recoil in low-to mid-level horror and disgust
and maybe even shed a few later when she thinks
about what's befallen her once-beautiful baby boy
(or, more likely, what he be fallen into),

surely the Old Man wouldn't begrudge me
this momentary indulgence or judge, too harshly,
me and the lifestyle that I swear I somehow
just seem to have woken up inside of, one day?

Surely he must have had a few days like this
special-air-drop-delivered from the wrong
side of nowhere to the ground-zero / crosshairs
of his world, back in the day when he
was a free-wheeling bachelor about town
(despite our fairly divergent paths,
worldviews and ways and maybe also the fact
that he was a charming, good-looking jet-fighter pilot
with the classic little black book of numbers and names,
a Corvette Stingray and a Jack Kennedy haircut
you could set your watch by).

Surely he wouldn't overly depreciate the idea,
despite the (very real and aforementioned) differences
in our lives, that it's just something you have to do,
every now and then,

to locate your zen,
center your chakra
and / or get your head right again
before paratrooping back out
into the *not my job / not my problem,*
I got mine / you get yours,
what have you done for me lately(?),
corporate, confederate, theoligarchy
of these Distended (fugue-)States
of AmeriKKKa, Inc.

p.s. They say the Lord is coming.

    Better look busy.

Drunk Directing Traffic at the Intersection of Time and Space

No sooner had I lowered myself
down into that dark well
of ghost echoes and distant whale squeak
than I was the poor boy of every
sad blues and honky-tonk song:

thumb out, on the Lost Highway
and a long, long way from home
(such a long, long way from home),

a lonesome stranger
hoping to hitch a ride
to ever-stranger lands (and
other Parts Unknown, as well).

I was Hank and Lefty,
Kerouac and Cassady,
Quixote and Sancho.

I wore the fabled Hubcap
Diamond-Star Halo and red shoes
that were the envy of every angel
(and devil alike).

I made midnight raids
on The Garden of Earthly Delights.

I stole Death's pale, raggedy horse
and sold it to a traveling gypsy circus
for pennies on the pound.

I popped, locked and moon-walked
in the middle of traffic
at the intersection of Time and Space.

I rode bitch between a mega-church minister
and a street-corner preacher on a white-knuckle,
cross-country pilgrimage to Nowheresville, USA
(my soon-to-be published account of my adventure
titled, simply, *From East Jesus to Hell's Half Acre
and Back Again: A Hobo's Tale*).

I got drunk on nine kinds of hellfire
and nearly died in a duel
over a one-legged ballerina.

I called out to you through
the dark winter forest of static
at the end of the A.M. radio dial,
waking you in the middle of the night
from dreams of butterflies,
coyotes,
wildflowers ...

If not for the alarm clock
pinching my ear with its
sharp, bony fingers,

I might not have ever made it back.

The Night Before Payday (and Exactly Five Dollars in Quarters to Your Name)

A tin of smoked sardines in hot sauce,
a baguette of day-old French bread,
half a block of white cheddar,
three quarters of a gallon jug
of what the label described, simply, as *Paisano*,
(and I won't lie, that sturdy, little man
has proved his friendship to me, many a time),
plus a jar full of fat Spanish olives
stuffed with garlic cloves and jalapenos
and one chilled black plum only just slightly
past the point of whatever this world might
offer up as an example of its perfection.
And maybe it was just the warm, sleepy
Buddha after-glow of the good fortune of finding
something where there could have just as likely
been cabinets and drawers and an ancient, clanking,
moaning refrigerator full of nothing, but,
that was the best damn meal I'd had in weeks.
Pretty sure I even managed to wipe up every
last trace of olive oil with the last fistful of bread.
For the rest of the night, as I sipped my wine
on the front porch, rubbing my distended belly,
watching the cars go by, I couldn't help
but reconsider (at least) some
of my (lesser) grievances
with the world.

Standing at the Intersection of Critical Mass and Event Horizon with Tom Wayne and John Deuser, 5:47am (or, *Hey Man, Is That an Accordion I'm Hearing?*)

A million fish wash up dead
in a California harbor.

10,000 cows keel over in Vietnam.

Thousands of Starlings, Turtle Doves
and Red Wing Blackbirds drop from the sky
in Italy, Sweden, South Dakota.

But elsewheres (and despite it all),
we've still managed to put in
another long (and more than respectable) night
of consorting with spirits and keeping
the Universal Kundalini humming
at that slightly heightened pitch (of radians
per reciprocal seconds) which has been
rumored by certain members of the tribe
to induce an *enlightened euphoria* of sorts.

And now the early morning streets (here in mid-town
KC/MO, 5:47am) are strangely Frisco / Portland-foggy
and deserted like one of those old-school / bad dream /
where-did-everybody-go? sci/fi movies from our
paranoid, cold-war era past.

Or so it would seem if not for the all-night diner
with its purple neon *OPEN* sign in the window
and the street light on the corner:

a peach-tinted glow hovering above us
like a stationary UFO whose (only mildly
bemused) occupants are, no doubt, wondering
if these three zombified monkey-boys
and their fucked up little planet
are even worth the effort.

And from somewhere
deep inside the fog,

a strangely musical

wheezing ...

Snowflakes

True night having finally arrived and settled in
for this leg of our long cross-country haul:
all cold, black infinitudes and Lovecraftian
expanses of time, the headlights of the truck
barely illuminating the road ahead,
no signs of civilization anywhere and I'd swear
the wind has been alternately whispering
and roaring its bleak sermon for days now.

And somehow I'm still working on
the same foot-long truck stop sub,
still nursing on the same twenty-some-odd-ounce
cup of cold truck-stop mud (funny how
with the right amount of faux dairy creamer stuff
it tastes faintly of burnt popcorn).

But at least that low-hanging cloud cover
has finally rolled on and the stars have all come out
and there's a guy on the radio now going on and on
about the various health benefits that come from
consuming coral calcium deposits (*marine grade,*
by the way) which apparently include (but are,
by no means, limited to) curing any and all forms of cancer,
living to a hundred and twenty years of age and,
most amazingly, the ability to grow a new brain.

And on that last, ringing note (with vivid mental image)
we seem to have arrived at one of those moments,
where, who knows, maybe the planets and the stars
are aligned just right, one of those moments when it's
perfectly appropriate and all right to ask of the night,
the stars, the spirits of your ancestors or whoever
may be sitting next to you, *what's it all about?*

As in the big *It*. The very *It* from which all rivers
and roads allegedly issue forth and, thereby, must eventually,
inevitably return to and within which all the myriad
archetypes and things are contained and are each,
in their own way, ultimately of and about (aren't they?).

And it feels, somehow, like we started out
on this trip weeks ago, months even,
the whole thing a grainy late, late show
starring some second-rate Hope and Crosby,
Laurel and Hardy, Martin and Lewis,
Kerouac and Cassady, but, really more like
the 21st Century American answer to
Rosencrantz and Guildenstern:

a couple of luckless chuckle-heads suddenly thrown
by wild circumstance on to the road with little more than
the clothes on their backs and the coins in their pockets,
more than just a little bit out of their depth
and out of step with the various machinations
at work around them.

But, now it's starting to feel
like maybe the wind is finally settling down, a little,
and the stars are burning even brighter
all around us in the cold night sky,
(yes, like fireflies,
like Christmas lights).

And then, from out of the murky,
under-sea-like darkness of the Illinois night,
there, to our right, by the side of the road,
a giant cross comes slowly looming
(and more than a little ominously) into view,

larger and larger (like the Death Star
from *Star Wars,* tractor-beaming
the *Millenium Falcon* of our rental truck,
closer and closer), a hundred feet tall (at least)
and all lit up with klieg-lights for what must surely be
the Lord's gloriously apocalyptical world reunion tour.

And now some British-sounding news-guy
on some other (shall we say more *standardized*
and *accountable*) radio program is reporting
live, from around the world (Greenwich Mean Time,
if you didn't know), recapping *a few of the day's
major headlines* —

*Astronomers say they've found
a miniature version of our own solar system
only five thousand light years away,*

*In Israel, a woman believed to be
the world's oldest person celebrated
her one hundred and twentieth
birthday, today,*

*and, for the first time in living memory,
snowflakes are falling
on Baghdad.*

Hey man,

did he just say
snowflakes?

Sleep During Thunderstorms

The quality of sleep during thunderstorms
((not wholly un-)like that which is to be had
in hammocks on late spring days
but instead, of course, with the obligatory
wind and rain howling and pounding away
at the house (if not the very foundations
of the earth itself)) always seems
to free the sleeper to sink
deeper and deeper down
to those primal subterranean layers
of semi-consciousness where sleep
is more like a ghostly oceanic underworld
and dreams are luminescent fish
skulking about among the weeds
and abandoned machines and whatever
other random little trinkets and forgotten things
that filter their way down there from the surface world,
down and down through the hundreds
and thousands of pounds per cubic inch.
And, sometimes, you suddenly come awake
down there inside the belly of a dream,
just lilting along on whatever
under-current that comes sliding by.
And, though you've become slightly
more self-aware (of a few of your
other selves) down there in the briny,
dreamy deep-down,
you do not
drown.

The Great Who Knows

Sometimes when the lone firefly
of a new poem suddenly winks on
in the grand hall (or one of the lesser
known caverns) of my skull
it's all I can do to close the borders
of this little back-water city-state down,
shut the air-locks and outer-hatches
and scramble madly for a pen
and scrap of paper in another attempt
to get a line or two down on this intrepid,
new visitor, this free-floating Christmas light
of an idea that seems to shift from one color
to another right before the *camera obscura*
of my inner eye, that is, before I get
ahead of myself and jump the gun
and write down the first thing that comes to me
no matter how ridiculous or underdone,
my jaw gone slack at the sudden *Holy Crap(!)*
and *Sweet Jesus(!)*-ness of it all (of which this
particular instance of the infinite
is just one of an infinite number of components)
and there I am, my mouth a classic simpelton's *O*
and out, out, out this little wayfarer goes
into the beautiful, wide-open,
mad / happy / sadness of
the Great Who Knows.

Goat Piss Into Gasoline (or, The Poet Tries a Tiny Dab of *Ms. Walsh's Bold and Spicy Sauce*)

She was definitely
what you'd call
bold and spicy;

a sharp-witted, multi-textual
and tangy treat for the mouth,
the mind and the hands as well.

Yes, a saucy, young gal
that'd tickle your lobes of higher learning
and pull your tongue in such a fashion
that you'd feel it all the way down
to the bottoms of your boogity shoes.

She was chock-full of crack-pot theories,
cayenne pepper and campfire smoke,
hoo-hah and hully-gully,
fancy book-learnin'
and country-fried anecdotes.

Let me tell you, brother,
just a few drops of her stuff
put steam in your stride
and strange ideas in your head,

turn a tickle-stick into a ten-pound hammer
and a boy into a man and back again...

we're talkin' goat piss into gasoline, baby,
goat piss into gasoline.

Still-Life With Dragonfly Perched on Beer Bottle

And here is a bridge,
not unlike a thousand other bridges
made of rusted iron and sun-cracked wood,

a bridge that crosses a creek,
not unlike a thousand other creeks
that wind and weave their way
through the raw fabric of the gothic,
Midwestern American landscape,

where a lone Blue Heron, maybe,
stands patiently contemplating a single gold koi
(lazily circling a pink lotus blossom
that is just now beginning to open).

And here is an abandoned barn,
not unlike a thousand other barns
in varying stages of disrepair
and un-making, leaning precariously
into the ebb and flow of the seasons,
the last flake of paint having long-since been
weathered away by sun, wind and snow.

And here is a country crossroads,
not unlike a thousand other crossroads,
where a dragonfly just happens to be perched
on the mouth of an empty Lone Star bottle
(sitting on a fencepost made of limestone),
and a hand-painted sign by the side of the road reads

SWEET CORN, TOMATOES,
WATERMELON 5 MILES

where maybe 10, 11, 12 cars, at most,
may pass through on any given day
and the passage of time,
without anyone there
to take the time to notice it
let alone be of a mind
to try to get a hold on it,

is ultimately revealed to be
just the slow, nearly imperceptible
rotation of morning into day
into night into morning

and a breeze
that never really
stops blowing.

I Can Never Remember Exactly

Sometimes,
when, for no reason at all, even,
I'll just bolt upright
(like I've been on the road too long
and almost nodded off at the wheel
and then suddenly snap to)
from one of those
deep-freeze sleeps of the senses
that the modern man-in-the-street
seems to be so prone to,

somewhere along the tracks
of my (admittedly extreme) elliptical path
around The Creator's mountain-top tower,

I can never remember, exactly,

whether I'm supposed to be
playing the part of a mouse
in the eye of a falcon,
a falcon in the eye of a storm,
a storm in the eye of The Creator
(of all mice, men, falcons and storms),

or, the *I* somewhere near
the core of a poem
(about a guy, by the way,
who's dreaming he's a mouse
(that's dreaming it's just some guy,
not a king, not a big shot, not a hero,
just a regular dude)),

a poem forever revolving
around its own foci
like a stake that it's been chained
(like a naughty toddler or junkyard dog) to,

a poem that, according to
the latest estimates and indicators,
will more than likely remain,
for the rest of its unremarkable life,

completely unnoticed.

Charles Simic Sitting in the Cheap Seats of My Dreams

It would appear to be
either a rundown vaudevillian /
burlesque theater, Poughkeepsie
(or Buffalo), NY, circa 19-twenty-something,
or maybe an old, black and white,
*recorded live before a studio
audience* style television program:

part *Honeymooners,*
Days Of Our Lives and
German Expressionist Cinema
consisting almost entirely of various
stock caricatures and other tragi-comic
grotesqueries of the perverse
projectile vomiting hyper-dramatic
dialogue at no one in particular.

They orate, pontificate
and gesticulate, magnificently,
without ever actually seeming to be aware
of each other's existence.

One of them is dressed as a World War I
Prussian military commander,
complete with tall, shiny boots,
walrussy handle bar
and singularly spiked helmet.

Another is, most likely, supposed to be
somebody's *booga-booga* idea of an ancient
tribal shaman or witch doctor.

Still another, wearing an expensive bra and panties
and a thin silk cord running from his neck to the heel
of the high-heeled shoe on his only remaining foot,
masturbates, dreamily, into the long shadow
of his nightly near-death excursion.

A chorus of mutts and street urchins
waits, attentively, for their cue (or a scrap
of food to fight over, perhaps).

And way in the back,
in the darkest and cheapest of cheap seats,
the lone, cigar-smoking audience member
smacks out a slow and clamorous

CLAP!

CLAP!

CLAP!

CLAP!

Tomatoes

The big secret is
that there is no big secret,
no code to break,
no grand unifying conspiracy but money and power,
and certainly no celestial shine to that
certain 1 to 0.01% of very often disarmingly
charming narcissists and border-line sociopaths
or their (most certainly charmed) lives;

everyone of us drifting, minute by minute,
closer and closer to that dreaded edge of the cliff
and its *(totally!)* X-treme drop-off *(dude!),*

out into The Big Who Knows Where or What...

The bright, blue wind that circles the Earth?
The white light of sudden universal merger?
The total blackout of unknowable nothingness
(by which the torments of the flesh and mind
must surely be rendered null and unto the void
and finally done away with for some conception
of the good, right?)?

Or maybe there is some non-corporeal (yet
somehow cohesive and sentient) part of us
that survives the death of the body and occupies eternity
in either some wholesome, middle-American
(and otherwise asexual) Hometown, USA,

or is, instead, tortured, mutilated and lovingly roasted
(forever and ever, Amen), presumably, because we met
someone's pre- or post facto requisites
for being a bad (or merely naughty or
disobedient) person

or simply refused (or never had the opportunity)
to sign on the dotted line at the bottom of the last
(of many) page(s) of the membership contract
to the One, True and Spiritually Correct Social Club.

Seems to me that the theory
with the highest degree of probability
is that we most likely come from
some configuration of dirt and to some
configuration of dirt we eventually return.

For so many of our fellow travellers through the void,
this rather innocuous meme (when you
think about it, really) seems to be the icy,
intrusive finger forced rudely into the tender, pink
sphincter at the back of the mind,

the first crack in the quaint, little
Christmas snow-globe in which they live
and which, apparently, must wildly distort
the sights and sounds of the outside world,
beyond the glass, in truly frightening ways...

No, it's not a hurricane,
it's just a little mist.

No, I'm not going to rob you
or try to indoctrinate your children
into the *homo / commie / atheist lifestyle.*

I have no desire to force you to *stand your ground.*

I'm only going to the garden
to get some tomatoes,

which, I would be
more than glad
to share with
you.

Mean Boy Looking for His Gun (or, Portrait of the *Word* as Muse, Master and Estranged, Non-Gender-Specific Lover)

Let's have another go at The Word, shall we,
my fellow frustrated tasters of the humble /
hind tit / squirrel pie of poetry (and all other
writer wanna-be types, as well),

those of us who sometimes find ourselves
standing on the verge of calling it off,
those of us just about to walk away
and find a new substitute religion (if but
the Great American Mega Church of Cheap Labor,
Easy Credit and Unlimited Conspicuous Consumption)?

Let's smack it around a little, shall we?
Give it something to really think about
and let *it* sob and moan, all alone,
late into the night, for a change,
instead of languidly lolling and lounging about
on the crisp, pristine propriety of the Officially
Certified and Validated Page

or prancing about on a well-lit stage where
people are at least somewhat nobly obliged
by genteel, bourgeois convention to
politely acknowledge its presence and
quaint, little *arabesques* and *entrechats*, regardless.

Let's be annoyingly coy and capricious with it.
Let's play passive / aggressive games with it.
Let's get it swashbuckling, snot-slinging,
knee-walking drunk,

then poke and prod it off the high-dive
into the deep end of the gene pool where sneering
sorority girls and high-end hipster chicks circle and snap
sarcastically at all its pleas and cries for help.

Let's call it on the phone at odd hours,
then hang up after the inevitable,
goddamn it, I know it's you!

Let's drive by its house multiple times,
making notes of the makes and license plates
of any cars parked on the street or in the drive.

Let's stand outside its bedroom window, late one night,
holding up an old boom box playing, over and over,
some of the things it's said to us over the years.

Let's all go home alone with a half-gallon
handle of Chivas Regal or Cutty Sark.

Let's watch reality shows where fat cops
kick the shit out of niggers, spics and white trash.

Let's scream at our favorite over-paid loser teams.

Let's grumble and guffaw and *goddamn right!*
along with all the snarling, frothing
voices at the end of the A.M. dial.

Let's play Russian Roulette
with a pillow case full of revolvers.

Fuck it.

What'd The Word ever do for any of us?

Chance Meeting, 3am

Well, here we are again,
wandering around in this strangely cool
tide-pool of 3am summertime dark:
just me, myself and my jelly-jar
of green tea and gin, a haunted wind
ruffling its feathers in the trees,
a plastic cup rolling along the street,
and me with a skull like a stone cavern
or shell whispering and roaring with voices
from the past, present and,
very possibly, the future, as well.
There is no one out here to share
the cosmic tragic-comical joke with,
no one to compare notes with,
no one to trade places with, maybe
(if just for a day or two and with
promises made that there'll be no
major crimes committed or persons
fallen in love with), not a solitary neighbor in sight,
not even a front porch light left on
for a flying Dutchman or ancient mariner
lost in the night, not a smoky wisp of a cat
suddenly drifting past or dog with tongue
and tail slappily wagging, not a wayward character
or creature of any kind, not even the chance meeting
of a ghost of some (recently deceased) second cousin
(on my mother's side).

Madame Laveau, Fortune Teller and Police Psychic, Begins to See the Light

Somewhere, out there, in this bleak,
little Romanian opera of a city
full of feral cats, rusted iron
and restless spirits steaming up
from sewer grates is a blind man
selling Nightingales,

an accordion wheezing out
a sad, meandering tune
from deep within the inner-most
recesses of strange shadows,

a wind-up submarine
marooned at the bottom
of a cast-iron tub (with three
gnarled feet and a brick
subbing in for the missing fourth),

a Punch and Judy puppet show
starring Mickey Mouse
and Marlene Dietrich,

a black votive candle (dedicated
to some lesser-known saint) burning
with a blue flame in a 3rd-story window,

a barn owl perched on a flag pole,

Kafka playing deep chess with a bed bug,

Tennessee Williams making small talk with an iguana,
a billy goat munching on a page
from *Being and Nothingness,*

a silver cat napping
on the bar of a hotel cabaret,
a New Year's Eve streamer (from exactly
fifteen years before) hanging
from the ceiling, almost all the way
down to the floor,

a man sitting at a table in the corner,
sipping Sambuca and soda (fleeting thoughts
of his youth like showers of shooting stars
raking across his mind),

smoke from a stubbed-out cigarette
coiling up through a red-orange spotlight,
shining down on a tragic torch singer-type
who has suddenly forgotten the words
to a song she's sung a thousand times before.

And hey,
have you heard the one
about the plumber
and the midget
transvestite?

Scenes From 39th St. Part 2

what's all this living for, anyway?
-ancient Sufi proverb

Well, here we are again,
drinking beer on the far, bright shore
of 39th and Bell (a.k.a. the palatial front porch
of Prospero's Bookstore) when, suddenly,
the rooster ring-tone of my cell-phone
goes off and it's mom calling
(all the way from Salina, KS) to tell me
there's a big, ugly storm marauding
our way (as if we couldn't see the signs, ourselves,
but I say, *thanks anyway, Ma.*
Tell Dad he still owes me a twenty for that
Royals / Red Sox game last week. Have a good night.)

But it does get me to pondering out loud
if this year or maybe the next could be
the year that the Hillbilly X-tian Rapture,
the second American Civil War and / or
that giant meteor people have been talking about
for years now (like a frustrated lover just about
to go crazy or give it up) finally comes.

I suppose, in the meantime,
we (meaning (this time) Johanson and Cunnyngham,
Whitehead, Leathem and me) should just keep on
keepin' on with our usual any-given-night-of-
the-week routine: talking politics, movies and books,

telling tall tales of wildly glorious
misfortunes and tragi-comic misadventures
from the sunny slopes of long ago,
gawking at girls (of often dangerously
indeterminate ages) as they parade and runway by,
even occasionally wagering on
the erratic behavior of cockroaches
to see who buys the next twelve pack.

Damn. How many years have we been at this?
How many years has some more or less
unwaveringly consistent variation
of this particular street corner court
been holding forth?

How is it a year ago feels like a decade
while some half-remembered something or other
that went down ten years back
somehow seems like... yesterday?

And here we are, the five of us,
adrift and bobbing along in that nebulous neutral zone
between *not as dumb as I used to be* and
some girl saying, *you're just a little too old for me,*
between the Bloomsbury Group and The Lost Boys,
between the Isle of Davos and The Island of Misfit Toys.

And, like the overgrown Peter Parker / college kid /
as of yet still undiscovered artistes we may very well be,
we'll probably keep on keepin' the faith for as long
as we're breathing (without tanks, at least).
And besides, what the hell else are we gonna do
with our time?

And, like that much misunderstood, much maligned
Frankenstein Monster of our age, Roy Batty, we will
probably be left desperately wanting *more life, fuckers(!)*
when our custom designed carriages and rickshaws arrive
to carry us off, respectively, to the Big Who Knows Where?

Meanwhile, back down here at the big pay-per-view /
pay-to-play main event of Just Another Friday Night
in Kansas City, MO, the crew has somehow
spontaneously multiplied into a crowd
and there seems to be a heated debate going down about
who would win in a fight between Magneto
and Doctor Doom.

And someone's pulled out the ever-reliable
Kennedy Trail of the Dead (and maybe even a little
something about the admittedly inherent mysteries
of Building 7) while someone else is taking bets on which
self-righteous, holy-rollin' culture warrior / rodeo clown
the Republicans are gonna be bat-shit crazy enough
to even think about nominating.

And the sky suddenly goes all charcoal /
horror movie back-drop.

And the thunder comes out
like someone's Strict Father Model of a God
took a drunken tumble
down a long flight of stairs.

And the first drop of rain
hits the sidewalk
with a sizzling

POP!

It

It is rumored by the elders of the tribe to reside
somewhere in that mysterious *no-go zone*
on all the ancient sea maps that reads
there be monsters here.

It scratches, kicks and thrashes
in the tunnels beneath our bellies
to remind us we're alive.

It jumps and skitters like dry, dusty leaves
across the cold stone floor of the soul,
sets a spell, then scurries away like a cat
suddenly freed from a back screen door, playing
CATCH ME IF YOU CAN!
CATCH ME IF YOU CAN!

It hangs somewhere off in the distance
of a tall-timer's thousand-yard stare
and routinely sticks a hard one
to the secretary of The Man.

It runs up and down the stairs
in our palatial time-share of many mansions,
a pair of scissors snippity-snipping in each hand.

It gleefully swings from the trees
and sees right through all our best laid plans,
best played hands and meticulously designed destinies.

It pays the rent, pays the tab,
pays the interest (at a healthy 15% I might add),
pays attention, pays it forward, pays it back,
and, if you're lucky (and I mean damn lucky,
like lottery lucky) It'll even play like It gives a damn.

It whispers hope into the ear
of the head that hangs heavy with woe.
It teaches us to speak in ancient tongues
and tongues, ticklishly, the ear
that will not hear the truth.

It revs the search engines
of the chariots of the gods,
idling at internet intersections
and high school parking lots
and then *WHOOOOSH,*

It's gone, baby, gone
like a murder of crows
startled into flight by a pack
of *Black Cat* firecrackers
or the *click-clack-BOOM!*
of a random shotgun blast.

Power lines and playing cards
stuck in bicycle spokes
and pork-pie hats sitting on freshly made beds
are very often vital components of what It is
(as are chairs estranged in dark corners
and hula girls dancing on dashboards, as well):

moonflowers and cirrus clouds,
little red wagons and red, rusted-out wheel barrows,
broken down trains and the ever-reliable
tear-jerking scenario of tears falling somewhere
inside an unexpected summer rain or busted headstones
in forgotten roadside graveyards.

And then there's the snarly, squealy twang
of a pedal-steel guitar and the shriek of cars
firing off the line under the neon /
Mother of Pearl moonlight
on a lonely two-lane highway
somewhere out there this very night.

And of course the big, bad monoliths
of Love, Hate and Madness
are all larger parts of the sum of what It is.

You can map the face of the Earth
with the latest satellite technology,
pick your way, meticulously,
through its gravelly guts,
sift, gingerly, through
the sedimentary layers
of lost civilizations and past lives
and still you grow only colder.

Maybe there's a requisite degree
of desperation or estrangement
to even vaguely perceive the slow-motion,
Matrix-style bullet trail of its passing.

And maybe, before one can rightfully summon It,
one must finally succumb to the hard realization
that they are but a baby lamb
lost in the much-mythologized,
much-poeticized primeval black forest
of the mind,

and the light is falling,

and the crickets and coyotes have ceased
their volleys of calling and responding,

and, is it just me,
or did it just suddenly
get really quiet
out here?

In Which Monkey-Boy Attempts to Go Toe-to-Toe with the Master (Round 1)

1) The only thing in the world
   sadder than a train broke down in the rain
   is a giant jungle bird, made of rainbows,
   trapped in a cage barely twice its size,
   slowly tearing away its feathers and flesh
   in order to free its mind.

2) As a matter of fact, tears not yet spilled
   sit in a bulbous tower outside of Texahoma, TX,
   waiting for the roving thundercloud
   of emotion to carry them wherever they're needed.

3) Having perfected yellow and red,
   and eager to begin with the fruition
   of his pallete and the subsequent
   coloration of the world, God himself
   hollered out a solid *GODDAMN!*
   and *HALLELUJAH!* when he finally
   discovered the secret to blue.

4) If not fairly evident by its flight patterns
   the butterfly is a being so free
   it may transmogrify into just about anything:
   a flying fish, a pair of lace gloves,
   a jungle flower floating on the wind,
   a man dreaming he is a butterfly
   (dreaming he is a man).

5) The condor (like the crow
    and the dragonfly), after completing
    its daily reconnaissance mission out there
    on the horizons of our lives
    reports directly to the god
    of the underworld.

6) Despite the popular misconception,
    the leaves of trees do not sleep
    through the winter with the roots and stones,
    but instead, one night
    before it snows, gather into one
    massive continent and blow away.

7) To be able to romance the clouds
    for as long as they have, the trees
    have had to drink deeply from the soil's
    dark well of secrets and dreams.

8) Like the smiling tiger
    or the rottweiler's sweaty grin,
    the ocean's laughter is best enjoyed
    from a respectful distance.

9) It is believed by scientists
    and poets alike that the hummingbird
    hangs its dazzling symmetry
    on an invisible river of ever-shifting
    coordinates.

10) The earth is merely *holding* the sea
while the moon is out
making its rounds.

11) While suspicion and concern
are initially understandable,
interplanetary kissing should surely
be encouraged.

12) A dictionary is a thrumming hive of words,
busy with the making of language.
A thesaurus is its nearly-identical twin,
buzzing with the raw honey of poetry.

13) The same department
that numbered the twelve grapes
of the cluster also numbered
the thirteen knots of the hangman's noose,
the three visitations of misfortune,
the six of The One,
the half-dozen of The Other.

A Day on the Farm, Pt. 1

It would seem
that Billy The Goat
is seriously cogitating
on the all-too
tempting prospect
of bum-rushing me
and cows are honking
on the hillside
of early evening
and cars and trucks
are reeling out a distant
and near-constant hiss
and roar on the highway
just beyond the horizon
and then, *HO-leee Christ!,*
there's this huge
Blue Heron climbing
up from a stream
that runs through
the middle of the property,
not even thirty feet
away from me,
to the first current of wind
strong enough to
bear his weight up,
up and away he goes
(and in no particular
hurry).

Every Other Thing

A bowl full of black plums and tangerines
sitting on the kitchen table
in the fading red-gold rotisserie heat lamp glow
of an August afternoon that's just now
phasing into evening,

half-empty tins of smoked oysters and sardines,
pickled peppers, crackers and cheese
and a gallon jug of homemade rhubarb wine,

two poets and a painter
(currently giving the guided tour
of his latest work), and now the old blind dog
is moaning at the screen door again,
hoping to go out into
the wide-open world again,
to be young and fast again, really,
to run wild with his wild cousins
who've been calling from the woods
for the last hour or so.

It's the same ritual every time;
he'll get as far as the tree line,
bark a few times at nothing
and wait for a reply.

Then, he'll turn around, dejectedly
(don't tell me dogs don't possess some rough canine
equivalent of dejection, let alone some fairly evolved
semblance of foolish shame), amble slowly home
(stopping once or twice along the way to look back
over his shoulder), then moan at the screen door again
until it finally opens.

And then, eventually (after a good deal
of serious searching for something
and sniffing around) he'll make his way
back to his favorite rug at the heart of the house
and proceed, carefully,
to turn,

      turn,

   turn

down the creaking spiral staircase of sleep
into what must be his favorite recurring dream:

chasing something:

grasshoppers,
rabbits,
dragonflies,
any and every other thing
that catches his perfect dream-eye,

through an endless
green sea
of wheat.

The Story, So Far
-with apologies to Arthur Tress

It all starts with a young Adam West and Eva Gabor
(having been cast, here, as a sort of flawlessly wholesome
American Hansel and Gretel) gathering up sheaves of wheat
in the purple-orange after-glow of a setting sun,
the whole thing set to a lush accompaniment of angels with
Chinese eyes playing strange, other-worldly instruments.

And now a tongueless dwarf (with a bright-feathered bird
perched on his shoulder) is standing by the side of the road,
holding, in one hand, the keys to a Chevy van (with a
valkyrie / viking princess air-brushed on the sides)
and a stained and tattered road atlas in the other.

And Johnny Socko and Giant Robot are finally done
with their daring-do adventuring for another day
(having saved the day, once again, from the clutches
of the evil Professor Hex and the Dragon Lady from Mars)
and are now slowly spiraling down into a deep
and dreamless sleep.

And Caruso, reviving his most famous role of Pagliaccio,
is giving voice lessons to Anne Boleyn (or is it Jane
Mansfield?) while some bit-part player (you know you've
seen her a million times, before) done-up in cliché
antebellum slave-girl garb is grinning a near-rictus grin
and beating out a jungle beat on an old washtub
and a tambourine.

And all the while an (as yet) unidentified goddess
or muse waits, anxiously, in the wings for her cue.

And it's hotter than a Mexican sidewalk.

And Time is slouching, leisurely,
like some rough, lazy beast towards
the capitol city-state of The Self.

And that crazy *sumbitch* Sisyphus
has had his sentence re-commuted (once again)
to splitting hairs with Ockham's razor
for all eternity (or just the foreseeable duration).

And all the while,
a butterfly sits dreaming on a railroad spike:
a dream of suddenly waking from a dream
and finding oneself to be nothing less
than The Great American Everyman,
who (it will eventually be revealed
through a succession of wildly improbable events)
has somehow come into possession
(one could very easily name it either a curse
or a blessing) of a magical toy chicken
that lays chocolate eggs covered in 14K gold leaf.

No one could possibly predict what happens next
or how the whole thing
finally ends.

Whatever *It* Is
for Tom Wayne

Whether It's the iron will
of the invisible, all-seeing, all-knowing football coach /
prison warden / stern, but lovable, grandpa
with magical powers that lives in the sky
or the slightest whim of the Almighty Illuminati,

the icy fingers of cosmic / Karmic irony
(probing the tender nether-regions
of your mind), or, the very *moment*
of which so many speak,
so many advise,
so many so earnestly poeticize;

that last, final, indivisible *whatever...*

Maybe this time thinly disguised
as a perfectly common word
in a book on Lipizzaner ponies
(or Japanese Bonsai trees)
found at a Goodwill store
in downtown Norman, OK:

a word you're absolutely sure you know you know
(or, know you once knew, anyway, maybe in some
past-life scenario, at least) but now seems to have
stripped its gears, dislodged itself and fallen right out
of the basic machinery of regular usage and instant
recognition altogether, forcing you to re-evaluate
your mutual non-aggression pact with all words.

Or, maybe It's a praying mantis,
eyeballing you, inquisitively, from your sleeve,
lightning shattering a night sky, again and again,
like a giant sheet of windshield glass,
a fortune cookie with no fortune in it,
or a fireworks stand that, upon closer examination,
turns out to be a small island oasis
of Mexican summer dresses.

Or, a car horn firing once
and then some overly precocious little kid
(your nephew or second cousin, let's say)
announcing, suddenly (and, to no one
in particular, by which we can also mean
to any- or everyone in the world),

E, definitely the key of E.

Or, maybe It's just a single sweat bee
lazily *perning and gyring* above a perfectly poured
and pristine pint of Guinness, currently sitting
on a cafe table in the sun ... whatever.

For many, a myth or, at best,
something one waits around for
like a cab in a bad part of town
or a sign from one of the many
One True Gods (of your choice).

For others, It is the object
of the ever-vigilant votive candle in the window.

And once again, It has come upon you, stealthily,
in a state of indecision, disorientation or bad faith
like a payphone ringing (with vaguely ominous intent)
by the side of a two-lane desert highway,

or a postcard sent a long time ago
from someone you haven't thought about in years,
found in a book you always meant to finish (hiding
for who knows how long under the couch),

or, as a ruggedly Hollywood-handsome man,
suddenly materializing before you,
claiming to be a U.S. federal marshal, and who,
it seems, is attempting to serve you *papers*
of some variety or another with a distant, empty stare
that conveys, somehow,

that this was not, at all,
what he ever thought
he'd be doing with the prime
crime-fighting,
door-kicking,
terror-plot-thwarting
years of his life.

Oh well.

Whatever.

My Generalized Other

I never knew what to call him, really,
never knew how to address him except maybe just
hey, man or *uh, say, I was wondering...*

Niether can I remember, exactly,
when he first arrived on the scene.
Much like our innate realization that, eventually,
we all die, that we don't go on forever and ever,
one day, he was just there,
smiling his toothy, confident smile,
drinking my last beer, wearing my favorite shirt:
a mildly amusing houseguest that never left.

Breakfast, lunch and dinner,
brushing my teeth, drinking coffee, reading the paper,
for richer or poorer, in sickness and in health, etc, etc;
there he was, neck and neck with me in life's suicidal footrace,
maintaining his *rightful* claim on me, my time
and everything I owned, thought or said.

I was never shown any references or credentials,
but was evidently expected to accept, without question,
my role as *dutiful subordinate.*

And though I could never prove anything,
(never actually witnessed any outright acts of subterfuge,
sabotage or character assassination) I always suspected
he was having a better time than I was,

never once telling me where the parties were
or letting me know what was so
fucking funny.

Madame Laveau, Fortune Teller
and Police Psychic, Hands Out
a Little Free Advice

To come upon a red guitar
propped in the corner of an empty room
at that exact point in the day when afternoon
is, officially, about to shift into evening
means you will soon be embroiled
in a scandal with a blue-eyed girl.

To dream of an elevator shaft
coughing up an ocean of blood is a sign
that someone close to you, maybe even family,
is plotting your downfall.

A noose swinging from a tree on a hill
means you will marry many times
before you find the right one.

A beer bottle standing in the middle
of a country crossroads means
that a decision of some importance
must soon be made.

To dream, repeatedly, of a votive candle
burning in an attic bedroom window
means you will soon change religions,
political parties or the color of your hair.

To wake from a dream of washing dishes
and find yourself washing dishes is a sign
that you are about to receive a large inheritance.

To see a telephone pole by the side of the road
suddenly begin to shoot sparks and billow with smoke
means that you will soon encounter temptation
you might not be able to fend off.

To see the face of your enemy
in the skin of a potato, in a bank
of clouds or looking up at you
from the coffee in your cup means
you should probably keep
a low profile for awhile.

To find a reproduction of an ancient map
of pre-ice age Antarctica
folded up in the pages of a book
on seventeenth-century French painters
means you will soon begin a strange journey
with someone you haven't spoken to in years.

Pissing off the Back Porch (or,
Golden Light in the Shadow
of the Coming Darkness)

Cars screech and growl
at the intersection
of 9th and Massachusetts
like juiced-up linemen
surging to fire off the ten-yard line.

A few streets over,
a crazed dalmation chases
the last Tiger Swallowtail of summer
through the late afternoon and into evening.

A train is sounding-off somewhere
and the tubercular case across the street
hacks and coughs and wheezes out
a *sweet Jesus!*

And me, I guess I'm just kicking back and *re-posing* here,
contemplating a lone sweat bee that is currently
circling a pint glass of beer in the slowly setting sun,

wondering who I'm supposed to be in this controversial
(but critically acclaimed) television mini-series we call *Life*,
what I'm supposed to be doing with the time
and the place at the table given to me,

when this whole thing is finally going
to start picking up the pace a little,
where it's all most likely going to wind up,
why we're all here in the first place
and how the hell I'm supposed to
get anything done with these shitty tools
and all this goddamn noise going on.

I mean, don't get me wrong, and all;
who couldn't love this life, or,
that is to say the grand idea, anyway,
of *the good life* that you hear so much about
and / or *living one's life to its fullest* (or even
just to its most logical conclusion,
whatever that may be) even if it is among
the misfit toys and banged-up odds and ends
and gothic ruins (of my, or some higher being's,
less-than-specified designs)?

Still, sometimes you have to wonder
whether it really is nobler
to constantly suffer the jibes
and slights and sick little jokes
of life's more overly familiar devils
(and mean, mistreatin' angels, alike)

Or, do you somehow contrive a way to rise above
the whole surging, slimy mosh-pit of it all
(the ever-increasingly toxic stew of it all),

like a flock of waterfowl taking to the sky
and just *fly, fly away, baby,*
fly, fly away?

What we all probably better get straight, though,
is that all our cryin,' pleadin' and bitchin' down here
at the ground zero of (very often) our own making
is wasted on dark gods gone (mostly) deaf
(and a little near-sighted, too).

Hell, most likely it all winds up
as dirt in the ground, anyway, for aliens
or future generations to find and sift through:
you, your family, your friends and enemies,
your cars, your clothes, your big flat-screen TVs,
your quarter-million dollar uber-suburban
warehouse / car-port you call a home:
all that shit you kill yourself for
that'll never, ever save you from
the ever-looming *reducto absurdum*
of old age and the grave,

every damn, least-divisible unit of it:
dirt in the ground beneath a mile-high layer of ice
the experts are saying will be on top of us any day now.

The best you can hope for
is a few good laughs and a quick death.

So, while there's still time,
maybe you should just go ahead
and throw open all the windows and doors tonight.

Go ahead and make yourself another Mai Tai
or Gin Ricky, Rum Runner or Mojito or whatever
and turn that music up, a little, while you're at it!

Drink one for fallen family, friends and enemies alike
and feel free to howl with laughter at that silver-dollar moon
('cause you know, damn well, baby, he's laughin' at you)
as you water the moonflowers and magnolias

with your grief,
your joy,

your liquid golden light,
runneth
over.

Kansas Clouds
in response to Andreas Feinenger's "Route 66"

They look like Kansas clouds, she said,
raising a postcard up for my inspection
as she emerged, suddenly (smiling somewhat
triumphantly), from a forest of t-shirts,
cap-guns, trinkets and toy tomahawks:

a strip of Arizona highway, 1953,
under a towering cathedral sky crowded
with cumulus clouds like arctic caps
that someone (mischievous) had set adrift
to wander with the weather,

their shadows slowly flowing over
the arid landscape below,
most likely unnoticed
by the hitchhiker
and gas attendant.

Big Shots, Bagmen and Nobodies
(or, the Day Dickey Grabbed
the Red Phone)
for Mike Jarvi

It all started out a fairly ideal Saturday:
no obligations to anybody but ourselves
and weather conditions that would make you a believer,
the whole goddamn world wide-open
with youthful hope and possibility...

But, somehow, we still wound up
neck-deep, in a big, steaming vat of
how-the-hell-did-we-get-here!?

As in some place we really didn't want to be.
As in *seriously, what the fuck!?*
As in the collective kill zone
of four military cops who've suddenly
burst into the room.

Scowling, no-nonsense faces: ☑
Hands on side-arms: ☑
Three shoe boxes full of weed
on the coffee table between us: ☑
Gentlemen, let's see some I.D., please.

And it had been such a fine day in America, too.

A glorious, damn-near perfect day.
A big, phatt fluffy clouds sliding across
an impossibly blue sky kind of day:
Denver, mid-September, 70-some-odd degrees,
and we'd only been there for a couple of weeks,
on vacation, working part-time temp-jobs in the day,
hitting parties and bars at night,
crashing at my buddy's second cousin Dickey's place

(who, by the way, had been facilitating
a *friends-and-family rate* / very close to wholesale deal
for us with this rich, white Rasta / grower-friend of his
for some kind of super-chronic-killer-kind-bud-
purple-monkey-sunshine-shit we were then gonna
take back to Kansas to disseminate for vast fortunes,
no doubt).

And it was barely even noon before we'd already
put down a couple rounds of fairly elaborate and exotic
appetizers and boat drinks at this Thai place
we'd just found that very day.

Then we did what we do every Saturday,
hit every used bookstore and record store in town
and then just go wandering around
some part of town for a while
with a couple of shorties, looking at girls,
lounging about on park and bus stop benches
like lazy vagabond princes going incognito
amongst our subjects.

And all the while my buddy talking
like we really were gonna be these bigshots
with all the rich kid / pot-heads back in
Lawrence, Kans-ass *(and all we gotta do is
make a trip to Denver maybe once a month
at most and how shitty is that? Not!)*

And then we finally get the call.
Time for the big *meet-up / sit-down.*

And so, here we all are now,
shitting gold bricks and sweating ice cubes
in this otherwise cozy office den (in a wood-panel /
big fireplace / animal heads mounted on walls
kind of cozy) at the heart of this massive, Bruce Wayne
type estate (probably complete with secret passageways
and a giant fortress / bunker deep beneath it).

And these MP motherfuckers mean business
and our young, wayward lord of the manor /
Yah, mon! / ganja king is suddenly sputtering
and overflowing with *everybody be cool,
everybody be cool, everybody just be cool!*

And I'm thinking *ain't this just the wicked stepmother
of all misunderstandings?*

Seems like this guy never mentioned to anybody
that his father was a four-star general,
a four-star general connected directly to the White House
and the Pentagon via the Bat Phone, here:

yes, the very phone that *Step On His Dick* Dickey
had to pick up and yell into, *if I don't have a pizza here
in fifteen minutes I'm lettin' the monkeys loose!* CLICK!

Seems like maybe this guy could have picked
a better place to *make the exchange* (as they say),
like maybe the mini-mansion / guest house
he lived in out back (or maybe that one just wasn't
wrath of Jah, jaw-droppingly, awe-inspiring enough, *mon*).

Seems like, at the very least,
he could have made it
a little more crystal fucking clear;

no matter what else
you do in this house:
raid the fridge,
rape the dog,
smoke the old man's Cubans
and drink his two-hundred dollar,
single-malt scotch,

you don't ever,
ever touch
the red phone.

Great.

Now we fucking know.

Son of *It*

Sometimes It comes to us
early in the morning,
just before the Boss Man turns on the big light,
or in the middle of the saddest,
most haunted part of night:

some kind of slavering,
black behemoth, from what little we can see:
all teeth, tusks and talons,
snuffle and snarl
and primal, predatory aura.

A lonesome and sorrowful thing,
that looks to be part wombat,
swamp gator and slithering bottom-dweller,
mandrill, bloodhound, wild boar
and raging woolly mammoth,

as well as something distinctly ...

other.

Sometimes It batters at the gates
of my brain with its great paws
and its battering ram of a skull
like the giant fist of an angry
underworld god, shaking the walls
of this remote, little city-state of mind.

Sometimes It just rubs its back up against
the great tree trunk of my spine,
thrumming and thrumming
with what surely must be the funky frequency
of warm fuzzy love,
or, at the very least, the manic need
to satisfy some maddening metaphysical itch
(his or mine, I'm never sure).

And, sometimes
It's content to merely loiter
and look on, inquisitively,
studying our most insignificant routines
from just inside the tree line,
just beyond the reach
of our guard lights,

nothing but your classic *dark silhouette*
and *glowing set of eyes* ...

But, of course, it could never really
charge out of that dark forest
of the wild night world of the soul,
and, by some freak cosmic occurrence
of a just and loving god blinking
or even looking the other way,
make its way into our safe, little,
climate-controlled environment.

Could it?

I Swear to God

sometimes it seems like
the goddamn cynics and nihilists
and various other strains of nattering
nay-sayers of hopeless negativism are right,
that nothing really matters
in the grand scale of things,
that there's no real meaning to anything,
as in nothing you do can really mean
or change or add up to something greater
than just a lumpy sum of parts.
Or, at least that's the line of (quasi) reasoning
I use, occasionally, to justify and / or excuse
those days that come along every now and then,
when you wake up around ten or eleven
and maybe it's grey and raining
and thundering out there, or,
better yet, one of those quaint,
postcard perfect / phone book cover photo
of a perfect spring day kind of days;
either way, probably best to spend
the better part of it in bed (just to be safe),
the shades pulled down most of the way,
some solo Monk or Red Garland on the radio,
a box fan blowing out a rough accompaniment
from the corner and nothing to do
but drink beer and write poems (maybe even
one about drinking beer and writing poems)
in bed all day.

Burlap, Buffalo Skull and Burial Suit

I suppose there could be worse things
(once you've finally released your death-grip
on the ghost, for good)
than being wrapped up in burlap
and buried somewhere out near the middle
of a great, big rolling nowhere,
beneath a big, blue sky piled high
with layer upon layer of clouds
(cirrus, stratocumulus, cumulonimbus),
a lone, old bossy for a caretaker, maybe,
and a buffalo skull for a headstone,
or, better yet, the seed of an oak
or acorn tree placed in the left breast
pocket of your burial suit (or whatever
you were wearing when your time came),
and you and all your troubles,
your ambitions,
your vanities
left, finally
(as it should be),
to the good graces
of the earth, sun
and rain.

A Laughing Matter

You know, even if this sloppy
under-age kegger / work-camp /
Animal Planet mini-series we call life
isn't always *a laughing matter,*

it's probably safe to assume that laughter
(not unlike food and water, friends,
sex and shelter against the elements)
is an absolute necessity for facilitating
the fairly standard (and increasingly common) routines
of Just Barely Getting By and Merely Surviving Life

let alone living well (as an end in and of itself
as well as being the best revenge, they say,
against one's enemies and detractors).

Probably best to have a reasonable goal or objective
or mission statement of some kind, as well,
to properly motivate and devote one's
ever-diminishing (by seconds /
by minutes / by hours / by days /
weeks / months / years / decades /
holy crap what happened to all my) time to,

even if you end up modifying and customizing
or completely changing it out and over-
hauling it a couple of times over the winding
obstacle course of your life.

And, who knows, that may just end up being
the thing you give yourself over to,
you know, the whole *living how
you want to on your own terms* thing
we've all, no doubt, heard so much about
(the laws of man and physics notwithstanding)
and shaking things up, every now and then,
just because you can and laughing out loud
as much as possible whenever you want
(or absolutely motherfuckin' have) to.

I mean what else can you do but giggle
and guffaw your way through some of the ill-advised
back alleys and gloom-shadowed valleys
that life so often leads you (by hook,
nose or cock) through:

the Modern Courtship Ritual, for example,
and all its many protracted emasculations
and demoralizations and exclusive invitations
to dine and drink alone,
late into the night,

or the requisite hand-wringing subservience
and / or cringing, cap-in-hand supplication
necessary to assuage and evade the wrath
of the world's various marauding figurines
of authority, or the repeated implosion
of everything you do to try to improve
your socio / sexual / economic situation.

And then there's that near-constant gut
-churning anxiety, if not full-on existential terror,
of being swept up and swallowed or just simply
trampled by what has often been (and maybe
less than charitably) referred to
as the *bewildered herd.*

And, of course, most disturbingly,
the absurd (though very possibly
unavoidable) daily exchange
of body, soul, time and happiness
for some sort of currency
(if not immediacy
or relevancy)

with which to then immediately about-face
and (foolishly) attempt to buy those
very things back.

How can you not help, sometimes,
but sit right down wherever you are,
throw your head and hands back
from the whole beautiful,
deadly, slap-stick /
tragic absurdity
of it all

and laugh?

And Still the Moon

And still the moon
beams down at us
like the atomically radiant skull
of a bald and diabolical clown
with nothing but dark designs
for this sad little town.

And still old grey dreams waft like haunted veils
and shrouds of smoke and steam,
in and out of the boiler room of your soul.

And still the psychotronic call goes out
on lonely, desperate nights
to moths circling streetlights
and stray dogs snuffling
the curbside garbage
of middle America.

And when the time comes,
the clouds will suddenly grow fat
and sullen as a storm begins to brew
its chunky mulligan stew
of fluster and flurry,
buzzards and crows wings
and the dust and clamor
of a million thundering hooves.

And there, perched on the hill,
just within the weird radiance
of the city's ghostly after-hours glow,
the lone gypsy-prince of coyotes
waits patiently for us, still,

like that near-perfect silence
and stillness of midnight
after the first heavy snow of winter,

like a telegram from beyond the grave
detailing the exact number
of communist spies in the House of Love,

like a recurring nightmare
of a man returned to shore
each morning (alive and well
and only mildly bedraggled)
by an ocean of whiskey
in which he wishes only
to drown the worm
of his sorrow.

Wherever They Stopped

By then all there was left
was a big brick house (still in fairly good shape),
the barn (barely standing), a few scattered sheds,
and, like a family curse or bad gene,
the decades-old debt.

The yard had long since been overtaken
by switchgrass and sage, the chainlink fence
slouching and sagging along through the seasons,
foolishly ineffective at holding
the slowly creeping countryside at bay.

The last John Deere, which, for nearly a generation,
had cut and re-cut their ever-dwindling acreage,
crawled away years ago to finally die
in a dark corner of that crazy storm
and gravity-defying barn.

And the old farm trucks, Macks and Fergusons,
in their time had probably hauled the weight
of half a million bales (or more).
Now, they just sit like the haunted,
weathered hulls of burned-out derelict war ships,

one of them run-aground and beached
on the edge of the south field,
another almost completely submerged
in that blue-green sea of bluestem and wheat,
the cab barely breaking the turbulent surface.

The other ones stayed wherever they stopped.

Mr. Heartlander, U.S.A. (Sleight *Redux*)

Hey, Mr. Heartlander, you're a busy man, these days; you're the salt of the Earth and the humble common clay, the grass roots and the strap on the boot of the man in the street, the selfless, carefree wage-slave to the corporatocracy, the backbone of the nation (and both of its firmly planted feet). You're the iron will of the plain and honest volk, the divinely rightful head of your naturally-ordered house hold, the capital letter of the law carved into the solid rock of the state capitol and the gleam in your eye is the gleam on the West Point ring on the right hand of God and, *BY GOD!,* you demand a simple, absolute answer to all the big questions (or, by God, you'll strictly interpret one for all of us). You're an unflinching resource consumer as well as the vigilant guardian and steward of the honor and wombs of all our obedient (or else) wives and daughters and you, your sons, your uncles and fathers: all proud, unquestioning fodder for The Great White Corporate Christian Cause, more than willing to sacrifice yourselves (and any others) on any altar that might, rightly or wrongly, come along and all to fortify the blue blood of your (super-)naturally pre-selected betters (which, by the way, as those very altars grow redder and redder, proves to be a blue, bluer than even your legendary blue collar). All of this, Mr. Heartlander, all of this, and still, most impressively, you somehow find the time, the mind and the energy to be both the mainstream moral-issue majority as well as a powerless, persecuted minority. Here's to you, Mr. Heartlander, wherever you are! *Cheers! Excelsior! U.S.A! U.S.A! U.S.A!*

Fine Day in America, Sir!

The two identically arranged characters
on the bus stop bench across the street
(almost as if they were attempting,
unconsciously, to spoon:
right legs crossed over left,
right arms stretched-out and
resting on bench back,
left hands in left-side coat pockets,
respectively) have begun the solemn,
gradual nod, jerk and snort ritual
of the seasoned drunk or junkie.

And another bus
has unloaded and loaded
and gone on without them again.

And a surly tomcat is strutting
and scratching around the scene
like an alpha barnyard rooster.

And a bull mastiff pup
strains and whines on his chain
behind the chainlink fence
across the street.

And then there's me,
just another aging, semi-skilled,
low-wage / low-status American monkey-boy,

waiting for my own ride out
onto the high seas of free trade
and competitive commerce.

Above us: birds, clouds, satellites and stars.

Below us: roots, pipes, tunnels and stones.

I kill my coffee,
light up a white grape-flavored blunt
and check the papers for the latest news
from the outside world —

among other things—

> *Swat-style "No-Knock" Home Invasion Raids*
> *Increasingly Popular With Younger Generation*
> *of Law Enforcement Officers,*

> *For-Profit Prisons*
> *One of the Nation's*
> *Fastest Growing Industries,*

and

> *George Zimmerman Tours*
> *Manufacturing Plant of Gun*
> *Used to Kill Trayvon Martin.*

Fine day in America, sir!

A Day on the Farm, Pt. 2

A grackle perched on a fence post
beneath an electric blue sky
where mountains and fat landmasses of cloud
do their continental drift thing.

Tiny sets of wings,
blue, yellow, orange,
like the petals of wildflowers,
flutter up from the grass.

The wind and the trees are twisting
together (like they did last summer
and who knows how many summers before).

A sparrow is sitting on the driver's
side mirror of a beat-to-shit pick-up truck
in the middle of a clump of grass and weeds
grown conspicuously tall
on a small square of the property
where all else is kept fairly low
to the ground.

Keys still in the ignition.
Battery still good.
Radio works.

Motherfuckin' Chuck Berry.

In Which Monkey-Boy Attempts to Go Toe-To-Toe With the Master (Round 2)

1) If you've died, unwittingly,
    and decide you desperately
    need to know the time,
    ask the man with the fez
    and the red velvet smoking jacket.

2) The sky-blue bicycle
    (on which so much depends),
    the one propped against the bus stop,
    where the old woman sits
    holding a clucking chicken
    in a brown paper bag;
    well, it finally won its freedom one day
    by simply being nothing more
    than a sky-blue bicycle.

3) The earth, in autumn,
    most likely meditates upon
    those things that only it knows
    still need to be done
    before it can go to sleep.

4) God doesn't live on the moon,
    but he does own a flop-house
    motel there, where for $35 a night,
    you get mirrors on the walls,
    Kama Sutra on the TV, Gideon humming
    to himself in the bottom drawer.

5) The Moon's giant sky-nets haul in
    its nightly catch of moonflowers
    and starfish, phone numbers and pocket watches,
    car keys, cigarette lighters and dashboard buddhas.

6) As a matter of fact,
    a growing number of scientists, poets
    and metaphysicians, alike,
    believe our life is a frequency
    somewhere between the violent polarities
    of sex and death.

7) Sex will most likely always be
    an admittedly phenomenal
    but otherwise futile attempt
    at summoning spirits.

8) Death will most likely be
    an entrance to somewhere else
    (hopefully not a waiting room).

9) When sliced open by the gleaming
    knives of summer, the watermelon
    is not murdered, but instead, finally set free
    to work its magic on the world.   .

10) The question should not be
    the distance in meters between
    the sun and its progeny of oranges,
    but instead, what is the annual output
    of oranges by the sun?

11) Sometimes a person's life
    seems to be nothing more
    than a footrace between
    the soul and the skeleton.

12) It is strange that we are not
    more shell-shocked by autumn's
    awesome explosions.

13) Spring is the golden-hearted goddess
    of beauty and eros that mystifies and intoxicates us
    with promises we know she won't keep.

Return of *It*

Maybe from under my pork-pie hat
like an explosion of butterflies and confetti

or from under the shadowy eave
of a barn like a squall of Starlings
taking to the sky,

or, from the far side
of the mysterious *Planet X*, even
(rumored to orbit the fading campfire
of our little solar system,
like a black ghost that stays, always,
just beyond the reach of its light),

or maybe, just this instant,
fallen from the pages of a book
on arc-welding

or hopping, leapfrog-like, from a cigar box
found beneath the floorboards
of an empty apartment
in downtown Sturgeon Bay.

Most likely, though, It comes
from that flickering nexus between 1 and -1,
between blind faith and forbidden knowledge,
between the could have
and the *Goddamn, I should have!*

But, recent studies are showing there's a strong chance
that It claws itself up each night from a shallow grave
that, years ago, It was forced, at gunpoint, to dig.

Though, rumors have been circulating
that It's available, exclusively,
through a mysterious import / export company
whose ads appear only in old copies
of *Club Magazine*, *Famous Monsters of Filmland*
and *The Savage Sword of Conan* (#s 134-151).

Maybe It's reordering someone's
prize baseball card or record collection
right this dark and stormy minute,
by the light of a dirty bulb
in an attic bedroom
that no one has been home to
in years.

Or maybe It's down in the kitchen,
napping in the lonely gap between
a glass of Old Charter, 10 Year,
and a book by Erle Stanley Gardner
(or is it the immortal Zane Grey?).

It flutters, moth-like, from dark corners
with impossible geometries
and the pockets of old tuxedos
in Goodwill stores,

from the yawning mailboxes
of abandoned farm houses,
from the trunks of cars
scuttled to the bottoms
of backwoods ponds,

from the jaws of skeletons
locked in closets
for telling unbelievable truths.

It crosses mind-blowing metaphysical distances
just to blow a sad little tune
across the dusty mouths of old beer bottles
sitting on fence posts and front porch steps,

or to throw itself, selflessly,
in front of an oncoming taxi
or east-bound Greyhound bus

so that some damn fool
(maybe even you)
may live at least one more day

to write poems,
pick flowers
or play video games.

With Its last dying breath It rasps,

Choose wisely.

Open Letter to Lucas Jackson

You sad sack of new meat, you.
You beheader of parking meters, you.
You malicious destroyer of municipal properties.
You unrecognizable pup.
You failure as a communicator, you,
    back-sasser, box-dweller,
    rabbit blood, hog gut.
You tireless devourer of eggs, you.
You kicker of bucks, you.
You chain-buster, gun-fetcher,
    natural-born world-shaker.
You back roads swamp-runner.
You good ol' boy.
You cool, cool
    big beautiful handful
    of nothing, you.

Laugh it up, kid.

May your mind never
be right.

Wherein *It* Conquers the World

It rolls with the punchlines
and bends like a skinny tree in the wind
to that point just before snapping.

It tips its hat to the ladies,
tips the scales in favor of the little man,
tip-toes off the tip of your tongue and swan-dives
out into the blue, wide-open memo-sphere.

It curves, effortlessly, into the helical turning of
glow worms and screw-guns, the pyrning and gyring
of falcons on the horizon and cop-copters circling,
ominously, above your neighborhood.

It will drop some knowledge on your dumb ass,
drop a grand in a weekend like it's nothing
but it will never, ever drop a dime.

It pounds and pounds on the door
at the top of the high stairwell of night,
demanding an audience with whoever
is in charge of this clusterfuck shit-show.

It carries water, chops wood, carries more water,
chops more wood, all with the hope of attaining
enlightenment, as in that big *E* Enlightenment.

It folds the space / time continuum from time to time
in order to bring two seemingly disparate points
of view together.

It occasionally uses a bit of information to chisel
a few bucks, here and there, just enough to scrape
together bus fair and beer money.

It lifts the truth up on high
then casts it down from the mountaintop,
tears it up, tears it down, builds it all up again
from the foundation to the stars.

It resides somewhere between *plausible deniability*
and *terminological inexactitude,* that sweet spot
between the unwavering constant and the ever-
shifting variable.

It's the broom in the corner,
the tractor hibernating in the barn,
the glowing tip of the hermit's cigar.

It's the sun pooling on the tree-line,
the blue moon in the window,
the classified section of a foreign newspaper
blowing along the docks in an icy grey wind.

It's the futile and eternal dog-tail chase for truth
(or its nearly-identical twin, at least), down and down
the spiraling / corkscrew snake hole
of ever-diminishing returns.

Whatever It Was

You know,
I'd think twice
about fuckin' around
with that thing
if I was you
said the old man
with the the eye-patch
and prosthetic limb,
as he eyeballed us, hairily,
from his back porch swing
with his one good orb,
looking like some
mad Ahab type dude
that, one day back in
the who knows when,
had just washed ashore
and never left.
But we all shrugged
and went on poking it
with our sticks.
Whatever it
was.

Consolation Prize

There was a part of me that, all these years later, still really wanted to read her the riot act, to give her the old *what for* and inform her that the faded lavender bandana she gave me back then (to remember her by, I guess, or as some kind of bullshit consolation prize, maybe, for not *qualifying*, hell, for not even being considered a contender or even a valid, bona fide practitioner of the sport), well, it was hanging from the rear-view mirror of my buddy's primer-gray pick-up truck and he and it and that damned bandana (that had, so often, tweaked me, existentially, from time to time, over the years, whenever it would randomly resurface to remind me how much she had hooked me and how I had barely registered with her) were halfway to Denver by now. But what would the damn point of such a petty little act even be? We hadn't spoken in twenty years. She wouldn't know what I was talking about because there never had been a *me and her*. Just me-carrying around the whole *what might have been* thing all this time, thinking that somehow, somewhere down the line we'd run into each other again. Hell, she probably wouldn't even remember my name.

Portrait of Old Man Smoking Cigarettes and Drinking Beer While Listening to the Cardinals / Royals Game on the Radio
for George McLane

A lampshade (looking, somehow, like a colorful,
wide-brimmed gaucho's hat, complete with dangly
tassles, even) hanging from the ceiling by an ornate
chain, its 60-watt bulb illuminating a kitchen table
where an old man wearing a St. Louis Cardinal's cap
sits smoking the stub of a cigarette while pulling
a fresh one from a crumpled softpack of Chesterfields,
pouring Busch beer from a can into a wineglass
from which he sips between deep drags and
disconcerting fits of hacking and coughing,
a Cardinals / Royals game crackling from an old
Phillips pocket transistor radio *(21 to 14, Cardinals)*,
and, over there in the corner, amongst all the dust
and spider webs and boxes packed full of who
the hell knows what, as if it had been censured
and banished for merely trying to do its job,
an oxygen tank on wheels, an oxygen tank
that if it had a face, would have a sour,
disapproving look on it.

Grandeur

The sky was the
whole panoramic
spectrum assortment
of Crayola reds,
oranges, yellows
and purples—
a pinata ripped
wide-open like
a giant ten-
point buck
by the side
of the road,
soaked with
gasoline
and lit with
a blue tip
match, and we
nothing more
than madly
scrambling ants
beneath its hot
and bloody
grandeur.
Or at least
that's the way
it seemed
to me
that
day.

Just Like That

This trippy old dude
always going on and on
to himself (or anybody else
he could catch away from
the safety of the herd and
skillfully maneuver into a
corner of his never-ending
earbud conference-call
with the universe) about
butterflies, butterflies,
butterflies, his shabby shotgun
shack (down there where the
tracks used to run before
the *government or who-the-
hell-ever* ripped them up,
years ago, *so's the trains
can't ever come back*)
full of cages of butterflies,
books about butterflies,
VHS and DVDs on
how to attract butterflies,
how to raise butterflies,
how to rebuild entire
butterfly habitats, even,
and the whole house and yard
saturated damn-near down
to the sub-atomic level with

the velvety, lover-like
flitter and slap of butterfly
wings, like this guy
had some kind of
supernatural pact with
the god (or more likely,
goddess) of butterflies,
and then one day,
while walking down
the street, pontificating,
no doubt, upon his
favorite topic, did, suddenly,
according to at least one
(mostly sober) eye-witness,
go POOF into a million
multi-colored wings
and was gone,
just like
that.

My Shoes, My Belt or My Haircut Never Got Me Laid
for Steve Bridgens

Got no fancy gilded pot to piss in
or bay window over-looking some
majestic scene to throw it out of.

Got no antique grandfather clock
to tell me what time it is,

no Teddy Roosevelt-ian moustache
or Walt Whitman-esque beard to express
my ironic sense of masculinity.

Got no basement full of home-brewed
and bottled cases of beer or wine made from
weeds and wildflowers from my backyard,

no Eurotrash wanna-be or fashionista-like
need to see or be seen making the scene,
no need to primp, preen, vogue and parade
my boheme credentials (beta-minus, at best).

I have no shame or need to defend my belief
in the profound depths, nuances and complexities
of an expertly crafted vanilla ice cream.

Though I will admit that when I occasionally
saunter and carouse about the town,
(a Hammond B3 and stand-up bass in my head
and my roving and curious eyes hidden behind
a cheap pair of shades), it is understandable
how I might be confused for a member of the *tribe*.

But really, I'm just doing my best
to make it from point A to B to C
(as inconspicuously incognito as I can be),
all the while avoiding the twin dueling
guard tower spots of Melodramatic Intrigue
and Law Enforcement, alike,

my mind fixed, less and less, these days,
it seems, on social media networking
or chance romantic encounters
and more and more on just
making my way home
(relatively unscathed),
one last drink,
a few chapters
from a book, maybe,
and an early bed.

LA-Z-BOY on the Front Porch

Reading lamp to the left. ☑

Side table with book and expertly crafted
    Manhattan or Old Fashioned to the right. ☑

Christmas lights left up year 'round and blazing
    like constellations of fireflies. ☑

Radio somewhere tuned to the classical station
    (currently featuring a solo for piano by Domenico
    Scarlatti, or one of that crew). ☑

The traffic and dogs around town mostly
    settled down for the night. ☑

The wind stirring the trees up a bit, here and there,
    but nothing to get too excited about. ☑

My God, it's all so fucking civilized.

Death Motif

I have often envisioned Death as a bullet
from a gun in the hand of some *fuckemo*
sticking up a Quick Trip at 1am who has decided,
suddenly, that he just doesn't like the looks of me.

I have envisioned Death as a pale, riderless horse,
without warning and for no reason apparent to me,
kicking my brains into next week.

I have envisioned Death as a carving knife plunged
into my pumpkin-like head by a woman who has finally
reached her point of critical mass with me.

I have envisioned death as a twenty car pile-up
on an iced-over highway late at night.

I have envisioned Death as an airplane suddenly
stripping a gear or throwing a rod and free-falling
into the ocean.

I have envisioned Death as haplessly bobbing
along somewhere at sea and waiting for one or more
of its inhabitants to take an interest in me.

I have envisioned Death as the edge of a thirty-story
building urging me toward it with my own morbid
curiosity.

I have envisioned Death as the gaping and jagged maw
of a Grizzly Bear suddenly appearing in my path
during a leisurely walk through the woods.

Death as slow-motion, mutually assured
nuclear destruction.

Death as inbred mutant psycho with chainsaw,
shotgun or fire-axe.

Death as incurable disease or serious injury
and me just another one of the 1/3 of Americans
without any health insurance or savings.

Death as a serious misunderstanding between me
and a SWAT team kicking my door in
at 4 in the morning.

But,as a matter of fact, I have never, ever pictured or
dreamed of Death as hooded grim reaper-type character
or devilishly dapper dude at the wheel of a hearse,
patiently waiting for me to get my affairs in order.

Your Sacrifices Are Greatly Appreciated

It is no great secret that the unrequited needs and desires of low-status drones (and all other various sub-stratum of ineligible walk-ons and aspiring would-be suitor types) are routinely and ritually tossed into the gaping maw of Love's not quite always roaring and never quite extinct volcano, as pre-emptive deterrent for any future uppity and insolent attempts at unchecked upward social / sexual mobility by the unwashed riff-raff from the general admission section, but also as genuine sacrificial offering to whatever dark gods who might be swayed into positively influencing the probability of another bountiful crop of beautiful rich babies as well as functioning as another buffer layer of assurance that the hopes and dreams and genes of the more desireable members of the hive are more fully realized and propagated. Surely, you can understand this, and your sacrifices are greatly appreciated. Truly, they are.

Still-Life of Pocket Knife, Carpenter's Pencil and Black Velvet Elvis

There was a wadded-up brown paper bag (with a few phone numbers and some directions hastily scrawled upon it), a brass candle-holder shaped like a chess piece (a king or queen, maybe, but the wax of many multi-colored candles had melted down over it, over the years, rendering it mostly gender-neutral, by now) and a set of keys that looked as if they unlocked massive doors and gates and gothic trunks and chests best left unopened, all arranged on an ancient card table (the kind you always got stuck at every goddamn Thanksgiving as far back as you can remember), a man, snoring, steadily, in a kicked-back La-Z-Boy chair in front of a Red Wings / Black Hawks game, a coffee mug of Diet Coke and bourbon, balanced precariously, on his slowly rising / slowly falling / slowly rising / slowly falling belly, (bloated with what appears to be most of an Imo's meat lover's pizza), a pocket-knife covered in red sauce and cheese, and the stub of a carpenter's pencil permanently fixed behind his left ear. A black velvet Elvis wearing gold wrap-around shades watches over it all and keeps him safe.

The Kind of Weed

that gets you to thinking that even though you've been drinking beer, off and on, since about noon (but hell, beer ain't really drinking, is it, now?) and even though it's been about 97+ degrees most of the day, and you've been out in it laboring away with your buddy, swabbing his house some godawful shade of atomic pea soup vomit green, still, a couple hits of this stuff after you've called it quits for the day has you, suddenly, reinvigorated and fairly confident that you can make it through all of the *Lord of the Rings* or *Matrix* trilogy tonight, maybe order some pizzas and invite some folks over, but the next thing you know is you've woken from what seems like multiple lifetimes' worth of the weirdest dreams you've ever dreamed: dreams as real and crystal freaking clear as your Hi-Def TV screen, here, dreams as freaky as any movie you've ever seen, dreams just a little too Freudian and Jungian to go into too much detail, here, concerning, and it must be almost dawn and you're sitting upright in the middle of the couch, clothes and shoes still on, a nearly full beer in your hand, tilted, slightly (at whatever windmill that has most recently appeared on the horizon of your mind) but still remaining somehow unspilled, a movie paused on the TV, and somewhere, birds starting to sing.

Preoccupied

She's the only woman I've ever known
who ever said she loved me,

and she said it all the time,

but never quite as convincingly
as when she was bemoaning
the latest disappointing *boy-de-jour,*
only just recently pulled from the
ever-turning hotdog rotisserie
of indistinguishable
softboi / art-school types,

the only one who really hooked
the old battleship chain
and two-ton anchor
to the base of my spine,

upon which she would (unwittingly,
no doubt) tap out a seemingly meaningless
Morse code of sexual polyrhythms,
from time to time,
when she wasn't otherwise
preoccupied with something
more engaging.

Gas Station Famous
for Victor Clevenger and John Dorsey

It was a Neo-Western movie of a hot and windy
Saturday morning in mid-September and summer was
clearly letting us know that it wasn't quite done with us yet.

We were buying coffee and donuts and DayQuil at a
gas station just outside of St. John, Kansas in a desperate,
pre-emptive effort to circumnavigate our looming
collective hangovers before they really kicked in.

I was wearing all black, doing my best working-man chic /
third-rate Tom Waits / Mike Ness shtick: big boots,
big belt buckle and paper-boy hat (rakishly angled).

Victor had more of a quaffed and groomed punk rock /
hip-hop thing going: red Chuck Taylors, baggy jeans,
a black stingy-brim and silk bowling style shirt showing
his sleeves of tattoos, plus just the faintest hint of cologne.

And John was just *doing John* as only John can do:
golden ringlets and big, bushy Walt Whitman / Taliban beard
(a few grains of powdered sugar here and there), classic
black-rimmed Buddy Holly / nerd glasses (with the obligatory
bit of duct tape to hold the whole shaky framework together),
and Doc Marten's with Virgin Marys painted on them.

It's possible we may have appeared a bit *exotic* and *outlandish*
to some of the locals who came and went with their purchases
that morning: *not from around here* written all over us:

and the three of us just sitting there, on the bench outside,
sipping our coffee, scratching away at lottery tickets,
trying to figure out our next move while watching a lone
tumbleweed drunkenly meander its way North on US 281.

Every now and then a car or truck would slow way down
to check us out, make a u-turn in the parking lot then
drive by again.

Hell, maybe they wanted to kick our weirdo, beatnik asses.
Maybe they didn't want our *type* in their town.
Or, maybe we just had the up-all-night / hangover /
caffiene / paranoia blues. You never know.

But we had no time for that foolishness, anyhow.
We needed pancakes and bacon, greasy, runny eggs
and coffee, always more coffee, because we were *on tour!*

That meant a solid week on the road and off the grid—
three vagabond, lowbrow *bon-vivant* Quixotes of poesy—
AWOL, MIA and *current whereabouts unknown,*
spreading the seed of The Word wherever the wind took us...

Eventually, the girl working there came outside,
fired up a Pall Mall and asked us,

Y'all famous?

Jason Ryberg is the author of fifteen books of poetry, six screenplays, a few short stories, several angry letters to various magazine and newspaper editors, and a box full of folders, notebooks and scraps of paper that could one day be (loosely) construed as a novel. He is currently an artist-in-residence at both The Prospero Institute of Disquieted P/o/e/t/i/c/s and the Osage Arts Community. He lives part-time in Kansas City with a rooster named Little Red and a billygoat named Giuseppe and part-time somewhere in the Ozarks, near the Gasconade River, where there are also many strange and wonderful woodland critters.

www.ingramcontent.com/pod-product-compliance
Lightning Source LLC
Chambersburg PA
CBHW030118100526
44591CB00009B/446